THE BEST PRODUCT OF THE CULTURE

Volume 1

Anthony James Godfrey

"I the LORD search the heart, I try the reins, even to give every man according to his ways, and according to the fruit of his doings."
Jeremiah 17:10

clfpublishing.org
909.315.3161

Cover design by Senir Design.

Contact info: info@senirdesign.com

ISBN# 978-1-945102-95-0

Acknowledgements

I would like to first thank Allah for a second chance and for keeping me in one piece as I completed these years.

To my strong, beautiful mother Ms. Lizzie James Godfrey, who is now up there in heaven/Jannah (paradise) with Allah (TA). And so, may you now forever more rest in peace. God bless.

And now my sister Latosha, a strong beautiful queen in your own right, a "boss." Thank you for all of your genuine love and support over the years.

And to my princess, my strong beautiful daughter Antanika who has always been my second heart beat from the very jump and to this very day. I'm still somewhat caught off guard, and I'm really trying to figure out what have I ever done that would be considered so worthy to deserve your unwavering, unbiased, genuine love, but just know that you have always been such an inspiration and motivation (one-love).

And to my two sons Justin and Marquise, I need you guys to always really look deep within yourselves and always try to become the best possible versions of yourselves that you could every truly possibly become. You're supposed to be better than me. Under no circumstances whatsoever give life to those streets; it's all false. And when you go legit, the sacrifice and accomplishment outweighs everything else. Now, that's gangsta.

To my son Lil' Anthony and to my firstborn Anthonisha, my love for the two of you will outweigh the bad times.

And to my first cousins Joey, Kia, and Shireen, I've really missed all of you guys a lot. So, until then, it's all love. I'll catch up with you'll later. Don't ever count me out.

And to my lil' cousin Emerson, everyone always looked at you as being a good kid including myself, and the few times you hung out with me I would've never guessed. I never saw that one coming (talking about you, because if I had, I would have definitely been straight on your head (no doubt). And so, all things considered, as an older cousin, I should have done better, but by then, I was already long consumed by the Black experience (the streets) myself.

Now that we know better, we do better- right! The first law of nature is self-preservation, and now it's blood family first before "everything" else.

I love you family; keep your head up.

SHOUT OUTS

A big shout out to my Belizean homeboy Big Hern-Dog (43). Always keep your head up, playboy, and when we touch that freedom again, you already know. Belize, here I come.

Shout out to my big homie Mr. Berttrain (B.J.) R.I.P. Yeah, my nigga, you put 43rd Street straight on the map (no doubt), and as long as I live, you'll forever be in my heart. You took me under your wing just as soon as I stepped on stage, and you passed the torch to me. I took it and ran with it as hard as I could, and I gave it everything I had in me. So, I can only hope I made you proud, my nigga.

A big shout out to my brother/homeboy Lance (Chino) Ennis. Our birthdays are only days apart (July 5 and 11, 1967), and you were my best man at my wedding ceremony. I think we have more things in common than not. I deeply miss you, homie. My only regret is that I wish I could've been there for you, but unfortunately I couldn't because they slid like 42 of 'em right under me, and so, I'm still walking this off.

And, a big shout out to my Belizean brother Gee (43), to Droop (watts-up), and to my nigga Cat (SBC). I got mad love for all three of you cats, and I consider all of you guys family (no doubt). Then, I wish for each of you nothing but the best that is one life has to offer.

CALIFORNIA LOVE

PREFACE

This collection of writings is a vivid expression of my truest thoughts. My emotion is raw. My mindset is deliberate. And most of my experiences you could say have definitely been shaped by the rigors and roughs of the black ghetto experience (the streets).

I've been incarcerated since 1997. But now, in these past 20+ years of my incarceration, I find that I am no longer the same person I once was when I fell. My growth is a complete testament that positive change can take shape inside of almost anyone, including myself, but you just have to really want it.

And so within these writings, you'll pay witness to some of my misfortunes and regrets, my strengths and my growth. And last, but not least, you'll pay witness to my undeniable gift of Black Expression in its rawest of form.

At your fingertips is the fruits that I have produced, and as you read, I hope to give pleasure to your spiritual pallet and fulfillment to your soul's appetite.

I was originally born in Berkely, CA, and at the ripe age of 9 or 10, I was sent off by my father's mother to be raised in Los Angeles by my mother's older sister.

42nd Place (between Avalon & McKinley Ave.) was the block that I grew up on, and the neighborhood that I connected to was ES 43 G X C's, and this area is known throughout the city as the East-Side (Evil-Side)/ or as "The Low Bottoms."

In the eighties, I was somewhere in my adolescence when gangs were flooding the streets and influencing every young and ambitious mind that crossed its path. I was a product of that culture mixed with the introduction of the cocaine trade. I didn't have any positive influences at that time to steer me in the right direction. Based on that experience, I always tried to make the best out of a bad situation. I was caught up in allure and illusion of that whole lifestyle from 1985-1994. I was in and out of juvenile detentions, Los Angeles County Jail and eventually, the prison system. I walked the mainlines of Pelican Bay State Prison, Corcon, Chino, Donnavan and Centinela.

Now that I reflect on all of the actions I have done in my life, I wish I had done things a lot differently and considered other options, such as completed my education maybe even enlisted into the service, landed a good job and eventually proceeded in a career that could have supported a decent life for me and my family.

IN MY FATHER'S WORDS

Well, it's been a long time coming, but the time has arrived. The time has arrived earlier than I could have expected, and to be honest, I know what I was pushing for which was another chance, an opportunity to be able to start over with you guys, but I wasn't expecting for it to happen so soon. With that being said, to my shorties, I can't change the past, and there are no excuses for my absence in your lives. But I will say in the time that I was trying to find my way with the cards life dealt me, it was like a chain effect because it had an impact on your lives.

I know that it has affected you guys in many ways because I was absent at times in your lives that you may have needed me the most, and it has caused some bitterness towards me in your heart. Please try to understand that I was trying to find my way. My decisions may not have been the best choices in life. I was using the tools I had in life. It's what I knew, and as a result, because of my behavior and choices, there were consequences, and I had to pay the price.

So, from my oldest to my youngest: Anthonisha Godfrey, Antanika Godfrey, Anthony Godfrey, Justin Godfrey, and Marquis Godfrey, I apologize, and I hope you find it in your heart to forgive me one day if you haven't already done so. I love you guys and have never stopped. I know that my absence has had an impact on all of you guys in different ways, and I love you guys all the same.

In closing, I'm grateful that Allah has seen fit to give me another chance. I feel that I have been forgiven and been offered another chance in life. In all the years I have been sat down or locked down, I have changed in so many ways: mentally and spiritually. I feel as though I am a better person now, so once again I apologize for everything, and I hope this is a new beginning for all of us.

Much love,
Your father Anthony

*Written by Antanika Godfrey

TABLE OF CONTENTS

My Best One

They say you never get a second chance in life to
make that first impression "RIGHT"

And so with thoughts before me and pen and
paper in hand then I'm going to give you my
best one.

Collective thought, compliment by free verse and
so this is where rubber meets road
(Real talk)

All comin' up, each embracing his very own
position now we all hold dominant positions
We LIONS NOW.

YEAH, I TOOK THE NEIGHBORHOOD BY STORM,
BUT WHAT I REALLY DID THOUGH AND
not even knowin' it then, I took the world for
granted.

Incarceration-political, prison population-industrial,
try doing (20)+ straight, on its face
Flat then get back at me.

Now, you tell me that you're still the exact same
person that you once were back then, and I

say IMPOSSIBLE.

Cats be like actin' and like seriously fantasizin' for
my life is a storybook of such still untold,
yet to be told, and truth be told I'll open up a
nigga's mind to contemplation.

Just know this,
I can bring out the best in the worst situation ever
and at the exact same time make it work.

They say that real everyday life is worth living for
now show us the dream and sit back and
watch us take it.

My struggle like yours then one in the exact same
THE COLOR OF FREEDOM.

MY AMBITION AS A LITTLE KID, THEN MAMA
ALWAYS SAID NOW SON, DREAM BIG.

It is said that the first law of nature of self-
preservation and let him who is without sin cast
the first stone, the terminology changes

Though the essence survives shamelessly and when
the rational soul is balanced then the
results become wisdom.

Symbols in Time "Reflections"

I laid down on this shit for a minute thoughts like
channeled into something else, THE PRESENT,
whole mind state like mind, body, and soul.

Watch me, now pay close ATTENTION to this here,
for the story commences to unfold.
I stay focused; I show no remorse, for this thing
here is bigger than you and me.

One in the struggle it was destined I was coming
conceived from my beloved mother's womb nine
straight months of total darkness, shit was chaos,
but little did I know then that moms was
already like a soldier.

From 42 to 35 life, 35 is my life, now on lock
like up in this evergreen state,
Walla Walla bound, level 4 max, 4 years closed out,
on point, ain't trippin', I'm here now.

The flame still burns strong, symbols in time
REFLECTIONS, I find truth in meaning.
One love to my nigga BIG HERM-DOG yeah my
closest road dog, we live and die for each other.
I'll see you at the cross roads.

Anthony James Godfrey

Cats be like actin' on emotion, impulse,
and clouded judgment, reactions
sometimes proven fatal, it's no mistakes allowed.

Now at this point and time within my life maze, I
retrace my footsteps, face my worst fears, stand
face to face
with my demons, expound profoundly on
demise that's to come, and also, I say a simple
prayer for those who are most near.

HOW MANY MORE?

I do this shit for recreation
For something like a sort of mental type
stimulation
Capture the moment/and make it picture perfect
In retrospect
Then it's a must that I serve this shit like
this for all of you'll
But most importantly for myself
For my little sister Latosha and for my big
brother Trouble
It's truly the only way that I could ever
express myself
Ghetto visions like a maze of triangles
And a 43-gun salute for all my deceased
And one love to all my true homies that's
doin' bids in the pen
It's TRAYS UP
It's no distinguishing between the pain
Because the game is based on love and hate
Illuminati makes all of the distinctions
Over precedent
While young niggas continue to fold
And are driven to their demise by dead
presidents
CAUSE and EFFECT!!!
Penitentiary steel known to break the most

realists of niggas
They say mind over matter
But it's like straight up time void of all pleasures
How many more calendars must I continue
to expound on?
And how many more ink-filled tattoo
teardrops must I fill my skin with
And how many more calendars must I begin
to count, that is,
until I smile again?

LIL' BEAVER

The list of R.I.P. goes on and on, and on and on
And every year, we rendezvous at the place of
death
We cry not for those that have gone before us
We only pay homage because respect is
mandatory
For we really cry for the death's that's to follow,
"Our own"
Fresh out of Y.A. (Youth Authority)
And like right back on the block
Drive by
No such thing as cease fire where I come
From only gun play
six shots to the head and chest
Now my young nigga is down
I hold my young nigga real tight in an attempt to
extend a certain type of solace
That only a mother's love could ever bestow
Thoughts flash before me
Visuals come and then go
Disillusionment
I tell him that it's going to be alright
That he's gonna make it
That he's gonna be okay
But when in fact in reality
Then it's really out of my hands

And there inside of me
Then a part of my soul slips away from
Inside of me as well
I stake my life on this shit x "10, 100' x over
That blessed is the absolute strong and the meek
And game tight is to Illuminati
Then what equilibrium is to like mind, body and
soul…

LIKE ON A FOR REAL SOLO

Visualizing catastrophe
Like waist deep up in this game
In the trenches

Armageddon is near
And it's instilled with an almost fear
That's imperturbable like second to none

Armor plated vest for my chest
Like armored down from head to toe
Stay ready for the war
Stay ready for whatever
Never say never
Because it's clear and present danger

On my elbows and knees
My only thought
Then is getting back on my feet

Lost and turned out
And like on a for real solo
I'm having visuals
I'm seein' doubles
Can't nobody feel me
But I'm still here though

Anthony James Godfrey

But if I die tonight
Just say a simple prayer for me "huh"
And let me know that
I went out like a straight front line soldier

THE LOW BOTTOMS

I came up from under the muddy water, that is, up
until the time that I was old enough to understand
that, then pipe dreams is a motha-fuckah.

Growin' up city life, then my area code being 2-1-3,
no role models in my life,
Only the weight on a young nigga's shoulders

Sometimes I wish that it was another way out, I see
the streets in front of me but I'm uncertain at best,
Shit ain't right for me and my nigga Trouble, and so
I'm going to give these streets my very best.

Now off and running for the chase, no finish line,
for it's never really any winners in the end,
for death comes to us all.

I've witnessed good solid niggas getting twisted
for the green backs, and
black on black then equals flat line like 100' X over,
and now it's three adult
felonies ain't this a bitch, all a part of big brother's
infamous plan to keep on setting us back.

Now I'm twisted and missing in action, out of state
incarceration like up in this

evergreen state, 20 years later in retrospect,
and I can still see the faces

The exact same ole once young niggas is now
older niggas and they're still doing
The exact same ole shit as before, shame on them
all,
for GOD have mercy on their
souls, THEY CAN'T SEE.

Once man child, now man, my life lessons came
way by exclusive like then the Hard-Knox teachings.
the streets tested me, and niggas from the other
side then they stayed checkin' for me, everyday
police constantly arresting me, but all along then
the penitentiary was calling out for me "huh."

While on the inside then defiance I contested, my
rebellion from within, all
along then stemmed from a much darker seed, a
hate then much greater than myself.

In the system, I was educated and taught that then
the first law of nature was self-preservation.

I studied ISLAM and was taught to speak KI-
SWAHILI,
MY CULTURE I NOW KNOW,

The Best Product of the Culture

MY CULTURE I NOW UNDERSTAND,
MY CULTURE I NOW EMBRACE,

I had to learn to decipher between illusion,
and then that which was right in
front of me, discipline we learn quick the
DO'S/DON'T'S, and the niggas
who got it comin' they get moved on.

But I'm ah stay a soldier that is, until my sanity is
once again set free, this
stronghold has got the noose wrapped tight around
my black soul, but if
nothing else then I'm going to be alright though.

20 years later in-retrospect and still see the faces.

I SEDUCE YOU

I seduce you time and time again with my mind,
I misuse you like, then
with the very realties of my life.
OUT OF SIMPLE SILOHOUETTE, THEN I BRING TO
YOU A MOST DEFINING MOMENT OF
PICTURESQUE.
Some things in life then on a much higher scale
than others, and in all things
considered then I solemnly baptize you the reader
then through my very thoughts.
You'll get a glimpse into my world through catches
and phrases, metaphors and
then the very outline of one man's strife.
You'll feel my pains, and I'll make you feel my
burdens you'll share in my story,
and if I should get too heavy on you, then please
don't misconstrue,
everyday reality then from simple illusion.
My every conceivable thought then is of real life
my vernacular then
Sometimes sick with it, and so spit this black then
from straight from the bottom up.
CALIFORNIA LIFE-STYLE then don't get it twisted,
indefinite
Incarceration, who better than me,
I can walk you through it.

The Best Product of the Culture

Staying true is all I know, then just ask the very cats
that surround me like on a daily.
You can place me in the fire like center stage,
but be sure and bet your bottom
dollar that then I'm going to walk right straight
through it.
Forever majestic in my ways, A SON OF GOD,
then I stay king forever.
And so,

**THEN OUT OF AMPLE SILOHUETTE,
THEN I BRING TO YOU A MOST DEFINING
MOMENT OF PICTURESQUE.**

CONSUMED IN THOUGHT

Consumed in thought now I can see the world
much clearly just as the world turns.
But of a future obsolete and bleak while
surrounded like every day by society's stereotypes.
Within the walls in my most precious mind,
fate is still undefined.
While I sit in my cell and continue to stare through
my prison bars.
Which are often times among others, still a haze,
and again consumed in thought.
I break the chain of mental strains, I consume all
pain, and then only strength remains.
Thought projection like more precise/accurate than
the bow and arrow of an archer.
Anger feeds off of the pain and hurt, which in turn
then manifest sin in the man.
Vision is blurred, thought projection now a haze,
havoc is reeked.

STRENGTH
STRUGGLE
LIFE
BLOOD
MY FAMILY
MY MOTHER
MY FATHER
I WONDER

THE BEST PRODUCT OF THE CULTURE

Liberation, free my mind, my homies, I still love them.
The ghetto, the games changing faces, having vision, love and hate. And yet still again, I'm consumed in thought.

MY SOUL STARTS TO BLEED

Thorn encased heart, my very soul starts to bleed,
tear drops running down
my masculine face, symbolizes the mere
pain and anger in my eyes.

Lord show me heaven's golden gates for within my
mind's eye, I could never
fathom with simple imagination alone.

Born in this world as a sinner and go
through stage after stage
I can look back now and clearly see
the years behind but not ahead.

To me the present is like a blindfold as I await
each new day never not
knowing what's to come.

Hypocrisy, false truths, broken promises, and the
white lie, consumed, enraged, compelled,
now I'm a changed man forever.

Defiant, revolution, the struggle, for my brother,
somebody tell me what's really goin' on,
eyes open wide now, now I can clearly see.

The Best Product of the Culture

It's black power when we holler, and so it's got to
be like black pride when we die.

ONE NIGGA'S PRAYER

Our father who art in heaven,
hollowed be thy name
thy kingdom come,
thy will be done
on earth as it is in heaven,

Lord, give us this day our daily bread,
and forgive us our trespasses,
as we forgive those who trespass against us
Lord, lead us not into temptation
but deliver us all from evil.

Dear Lord, holler at me if you hear me,
because I'm compelled by mere emotions
alone to simply put together another piece,
and guess what
then this one is especially for you.

Dear Lord, I got another letter in the mail like
just the other day,
and from reading between the lines,
I don't think my big brother is out there living right,
and there's something in the back of my
mind subconsciously
that just keeps telling me that
he's like falling off,

THE BEST PRODUCT OF THE CULTURE

and there is absolutely nothing that I can do
to make this right,
sleepless nights and one's own plight,
which leads me to think ahead like 5 or 10 yrs. from
now
I wonder what's to come.

My tears commence to fall down almost like
mechanical,
because the hurt, the thought, then the pain of it
all
can oftentimes be unbearable,
simply to the point that I'm forced to close
my mind,
and shut my eyes to simply block it all out

Dear Lord, only you can make this right,
I'll give you my life,
show me heaven's golden gates
for deep down inside, I know that I am my
brother's keeper.

HAITI

I never knew you until today, and you don't know
me, but my skin be black the exact same as yours.

My heart cries out; my thoughts become uneasy;
my inner spirit now wants to like literally break free
from my steel cage and fly high
Then, all I could ever do is extend a strong
masculine
hand and a most solemn prayer.

She was buried alive for six days straight, and when
the cement blocks were
lifted up off her shoulders, her very first words to
the world were:
"DON'T EVER BE AFRAID OF DEATH."
Now how strong in faith is this?

WE LOVIN' HAITI
IS YOU LOVIN' HAITI?

Sometimes, I just look around me, I stop and stare
at nothing in particular.
The world before me yeah, it's been a long time
now, separated from my shorties
And often times what I saw then is
everything on the bottom.

I fight hard to hold back the pain which seldom
tries to break free from my immaculate eyes.
I regroup; I shake it off; I bite down hard on it,
now I'm right back focused.

WE LOVIN' HAITI
IS YOU LOVIN' HAITI?

Innocent little souls then could only ever cry out
for the security and sanctity of their mother's love.

Then, all the while straight-up knocking on
heaven's door.
Time is fast running out, they breath no more, first
response teams never
there quick enough, the Haitian experience 7.0.

Bodies literally scattered like all throughout the
streets heap upon heaps,
200,000+ strong, have you ever paid witness to
mass graves?
A real-life reality twist, no ROB ZOMBIE Hollywood
type of get down here
Man, I tell ya now how much more realer does this
one life of ours get.

Tsunami in Asia, wildfires in California, war
indefinite like all throughout the Middle East.

A hurricane Katrina is to New Orleans what
a 7.0 was to Haiti.

Destruction, suffering, beyond comprehension,
death is the one price that we
have to pay for living, some say this be the very
nature of things, while some
would hold that then this be the divine law, the
decree of ALLAH'S everything.

And while some could only ever truly hope for the
basics/simple necessities of
life, then with many it seems to be always never
enough "then it's always something."

For the strength in the Haitian people is like
through and through in their pride and
their resilience, and if you listen closely, you can
even hear it also in their chants and in their songs.

**I'M FEELIN' HAITI
IS YOU FEELIN' HAITI?**

HOW CAN I TRUST YOU?

What confidence can be born of a bond between
men,
in what world could
such an alliance be considered stable?
Did not Eve betray Adam in committing the first
sin?
Did not Cain raise his hand against his own brother
Abel?
How many times have we put blind faith in a
leader?
How often have you?
Spoken up, and stood for the good of the masses.

Do you remember how men repaid their great
Caesar?
Did you not pay attention?
In your history classes, were we traitors to England
or patriots of America?

What of the treatment of the Africans, Asians, and
Natives, the implications?
Should cause worldwide hysteria, it would seem all
mankind are masochists and sadists,
Words like biological, chemical, and nuclear
weapons, are we really so civilized, are we really so
savage.

Am I my brother's keeper? The age old question,
answered by terrorist's attacks
And collateral damage, men killed Malcom and
Martin Luther King, Jr.
Persecuted the likes of Muhammad and Gandhi

The blood of the innocent who have been
needlessly slaughtered, continue to
torture and haunt me, even our almighty GOD was
betrayed by Lucifer's evil,
Jesus was sent to redeem us, and he was betrayed
by his own people.

Pledge of oath on your honor is what you swear,
have hope, have faith, I won't
abandon you is what's declared, you say
trickeration, and machination have
not corrupted you, but if GOD can't trust his own
creation then how could I ever trust you.

Alpha & Omega

The Alpha and then the Omega, life and then death, are one in the exact same because the two go hand in hand.

For a child is born into total darkness, and now from a most sacred womb then light is shown.

Now screaming population control, they are steady regulating the pill,

Contraceptives equal alternative measures, now got my sisters tying their tubes for fear of a much stronger black nation.

HARRIET TUBMAN. SORJOURNER TRUTH. CORETTA SCOTT KING. ELAINE BROWN. ANGELA DAVIS. ASATA SUKUR. WINNIE MANDELA. Just to name a few, now tell me they ain't strong

Now in these present and not so pleasant modern day times somebody tell me then where do we go from here SAVE FACE.

Now on lock as I stare through prison bars, profound thoughts channel my every focus, got me now contemplating my very own survival.

Because along the way being brought up with a wool draped over my face, all I had was mama's love nothing else, now who's the blame.

I now go through a metamorphous state, the
streets keep calling, I call back, now I find myself
totally consumed in misplaced hate.

For heaven's sake JAH, please rain down on me
your most truest of love and mercy, for I confess
my faults.

For a child is born into total darkness, and now
from a most sacred womb then light is shown.

ARE YOU STILL THERE?

MY THOUGHTS REFLECT, MY MIND WONDERS,
LITTLE BLACK CHILD ARE YOU STILL WITH ME,
WHERE YOU AT, ARE YOU STILL THERE?

From day to day I keep on singing, I sing another
song praying for a much brighter tomorrow, while
trapped inside of this maze, within the bowels of
the
belly of the beast.

Mind strong, stay strong, then staying a soldier is
my daily bread, my one and only sustenance, and
so I keep on pushin' trying to flip another
tomorrow.

Can't expound on how I keep on holding on, but it
got to be something greater than self, because now
that I think about it, I don't really want to die.

Ghetto visions equal pipe dreams, little black child
runnin' wild then makes for straight up lost and
turned out, crack fiends now real live demons,
stick-up kid, now gunman, now doin' 25 with and L.

Now big brother/little brother, when reached full
adulthood then who will become the strongest,
little brother become the strongest, and consumes
all of the pain, as though carrying the weight of an
entire generation of people on his shoulders.

Mamma, where you at? Are you near me?
Can you feel me? Then, if a presence is felt, why
don't you say a little prayer for me, huh?
Because of how one stay so strong is of no secret,
one must whole heartedly embrace the love of the
game, as equally, then with the love and pain.

Reflect on hurt, reflect on the despair, respect the
lives which are given, respect the dead, because
they who've reached the epitome, reach the cross
roads.

MY THOUGHTS REFLECT, MY MIND WONDERS,
LITTLE BLACK CHILD ARE YOU STILL WITH ME?
WHERE YOU AT? ARE YOU STILL THERE?

I Fear Not

ILLUMINATI, we got to bring them down, the definition of equilibrium is balance, like mind, body, and soul.

They say blessed is the absolute strong and the meek, but just how long is it gonna take though?

I say break the chains, erase the pains, eradicate the fears, no more tears, no more heartaches.

Post mordem when we die, evolution when we live, accepting ALLAH is everlasting life, perception brings about change, and knowing of oneself brings complete understanding.

I FEAR NOT

And when I die, I die for the struggle, because now I understand self, since I've been gone now my big brother's head is all fucked-up, twisted mentally.

And me and the moms was never really afforded that mother to son relationship,
Separated as a child, now man-child doin' like 40+

I look to the heavens and the earth for a sign,
any sign,
but when I look through my

minds-eye, then all I can see is the struggle, the
ghetto, and the pain in my little sister's eyes, and I
can only sit
back and watch, as my brother continues to go
through life with his eyes closed.

I FEAR NOT

BLACK HISTORY/ 2013

Reality/Check, On point with it/Check, real-life
illustrations, and from a most realistic
and spiritual standpoint then was all here on
borrowed time, BELIEVE THAT, From Adam the first
prophet to MUHAMMAD the last messenger to
GOD we belong, and to him, we all shall return.

MY THOUGHTS READ MORE LIKE A COURSE
CATALOG THAN JUST SOMETHING OUT
OF THE NORM.

BLACK LIFE IRREPLACEABLE,
BLUE BLOOD PEDIGREE,
AND NOW I'M ABOUT TO COME STRAIGHT
UNGLUED ON THIS ONE.

What comes from the heart speaks to the heart,
and what's already been tried is not always true,
sins of the father/ now inherited by the son,
plantation politics/
best forgotten.

My theme is based on everyday real life; my get
down is something of an ANOMALY of the sort,
place me in my cipher; now watch me put my best
foot forward.

Many shades of grey, but then it always seems to
come back around to either White or Black.

Human nature becomes distorted by the many
faces of man; the law of attraction then doesn't get
it twisted for a thing is ever seldom than what it
really appears to be.
Abject poverty, then directly connect to universal
oppression than my most truest thoughts, now
bleed black ink all over these pages.

I splash cold hard reality into the faces of those
who doubt somebody give me

A steady drumbeat, then couples with a strong
sense of black African Pride, and

I'll give you all of me/transparent, in the true
likeness of BLOOD, SWEAT, and TEARS, MIND,
BODY,
and SOUL for real.

Not the heavens/nor GOD shed tears for me,
everyday trial by fire, lessons in life learned the
hard way, then in the end,
each man made to stand before GOD alone.

MY THOUGHTS READ MORE LIKE A COURSE
CATALOGUE- THAN AS JUST SOMETHING OUT OF
THE NORM

BLACK LIFE/IRREPLACEABLE, BLUE BLOOD
PEDIGREE, AND NOW I'M ABOUT TO COME
STRAIGHT
UNGLUED ON THIS ONE.

Each day is supposed to be a treasured gift, then
it's always room for improvement and growth to
evolve to a higher and better state.

Your future is created by what you do today/not
tomorrow, and be open to all of the possibilities of
your life, for the subject doesn't really matter, for
it's really the process of learning and living that
counts the most in life.

ANTANIKA

When you feel that you're forgotten or confused
about who's watching, questioning if anyone
remembers,

KEEP HOLDING UP

In my heart there lies a place until we meet face to
face, where I hold onto
Remembrance of my father, a man's whose great

KEEP HOLDING UP

The past is long gone, and in your heart, you may
feel wrong, but in reality
your position is far greater than to hear you're
gone, a man that held his family up, a soldier that
never gave up, and when life took its twists, you
were still standing up

KEEP HOLDING UP

It's easy to say or to think about what you didn't
do, but as my father, I say thank you, because I am
here, and it is because of you, and for that I love
you.

KEEP HOLDING UP

THE BEST PRODUCT OF THE CULTURE

So many people you provide for, a spirit of GOD anyone could ask for, everything in life was predestined, so remember that when you begin to question, yes there are things in life you may feel haven't taken place, or the father you desired to be just didn't take place, remember that GOD is in control, that's what is so great, every thought, tear and even the concerns that were in question, God is going to work it all out, he is the master of all blessings

KEEP HOLDING UP

So, I encourage you and strengthen you to keep holding up, and to continue fighting because your race is not up, just

KEEP HOLDING UP

In due time, every question that is unanswered and every heart of forgiveness
will have its answer, GOD knows and looks at the heart of every man.
With Jehovah in your corner, did you know you already win, so no worries, no pain, and no doubts because there will be a change.

KEEP HOLDING UP

Everything in life that took place was not a mistake,
yes choices that were made may not have been so
great, but remember only GOD can judge you,
that's what I always say,

KEEP HOLDING UP

The moon and the sun still sit in the same place;
roosters still crow at 6am in the morning.
The sky is still blue, and yes, traffic still clogs up
the streets of L.A.
Although your physical appearance is not present,
your spiritual presence is a blessing.

KEEP HOLDING UP

Until we meet face to face, stand strong as
you run your race and remember

KEEP HOLDING UP

By Antanika Godfrey

MAMA

Mama, you gave me life
And that's more than any son or
Daughter can ask for
Like a lioness to her cubs
You nurtured and protected me
That is, up until I was strong enough

And even though I was a little bitty nigga
I silently made a promise to myself that
When I got old enough
That I would do the exact same for you

Now this late in the game
The game changed faces
I'm sorry and broken-hearted, Mama
Because now my one and only dream
Has been shattered like broken glass
And so it now might be a promise that I
Won't be able to keep

But my one and only wish is that
That you could see me now
In my full glory
And in my full adulthood state of being
Handsome as ever
Charming and mystique

And really feeling my powers

A long way from the man-child I once was
Now shaped and molded
By the rigors and roughs of the ghetto
Stronghold
BLUE PENITENTIARY STEEL
And this present modern day
Socioeconomic twist

I've been shaped by all the weathers of
This storm
Sometimes ruthless
Oftentimes heartless
Now emotionally number from all emotion
Mama, I'm now a SOLDIER.

"R.I.P. Momma"
Lizzie "Jane" Godfrey
1949-2013

A Page for My Mama

R.I.P. Mama
Lizzie "Jane" Godfrey
1949-2013

Dear Judge Adams,

I would first like to start off by offering the following to the family of Carlos CJ Villamore: I have searched every part of my being on how to show my deepest regrets and apologies for what I have done, and there are not any words to express my sincere remorse to the degrees of loss for the weight of my past choices, which are heavy on my chest daily, but I know that it is no way in comparison to the pain and anguish I have caused to the Villamore family. In understanding there is nothing that I can say or do to remedy the harm I have caused, I only hope that in seeking the mercy of the court that I am not causing you more pain than you already feel.

In 1997, I made a series of choices that irreparably harmed your family. Regrettably, upon moving to Washington from California, I remained in the gang and drug dealing environment that I hoped to escape. On the night of the murder, I threatened Mr. Villamore with a gun. I joined Mr. Ramos in searching for Villamore, and I shot and killed Mr. Villamore. I desperately wish I had made just one different choice that night, but I did not, and I will live with this for the rest of my life.

To Judge Adams, I thank you for giving me the opportunity to speak with you today and share how in the past 23 years, I have grown and evolved into a completely different person than when I entered prison.

I never thought that there would be a day that my thoughts and feelings for over these past 20+ years would be the billboard of my hope for relief, and it wasn't until I completely humbled myself to the understanding of servitude for others that I began to appreciate the value of all living things. God Himself could even bear witness to this truth, yet this is about me giving the opportunity to sincerely show you that I have evolved to someone better than I was a long time ago.

In seeking the mercy of the court, in no way do I seek to minimize the crime I committed nor the pain and suffering I caused. I am not seeking to avoid the consequences of my choices. Instead, I hope to convey to you just how deeply I understand the harm my choices and actions caused and how I have used every minute of every day in prison to become the person I am today. A person who now holds accountability in the highest regard.

Based on my introspection, I sincerely understand why the justice system needs prosecutors. I just want to make it clear that I fully and completely appreciate your position. I was no good to anyone, not even to myself. The fact of the matter is your civic duty to uphold the law and public safety establishes a virtue that is an essential part of the justice system. You did society and myself a good deed by my conviction, for being incarcerated forces a person to reflect on his life. Some of us take heed to the error of our ways and some don't and that's why it's necessary for me to take the appropriate steps. It's sad to mention but this is what it took for me to understand the value of life, family. and self. I am so regretful for what I have done, and I am in a great deal of debt to society from here on out. It has become a big part of me with every God-given breath to always recognize and make a conscious effort to give back.

During my time here at SCCC, while programming out in correctional industries, I signed up to take a communication class they had made available to us and to me personally. What I found to be the one most interesting thing about that curriculum was that it spoke to me and it explained in detail the difference between a FIXED MINDSET/ AND A GROWTH MINDSET, and right then and there, something about my past and the way I lived my life clicked.

In hindsight, for the better part of my life, I now understand that I carried around a fixed mindset and my real transformation and growth had really begun to take shape and manifest itself sometime after my first four years of incarceration, and to somewhat understand my actions on April 18, 1997, then you would also have to factor in and take into account the root cause of my mindset at that time, which led up to this point in my life.

I was brought up in an environment and in a time around individuals and influences that encouraged bad behavior, and realistically, statistics show that I'm not even supposed to be here right now, and so now when I really look at it for what it is, then in my past life, I was only existing because the manner in which I was brought up in wasn't really living at all. I came from a place where negativity not only affected me, but it impacted the world over and so it's hard to value life when you don't know the value of your own life and also the value of life where each human being is concerned.

In regards to my new reformed lifestyle change, I have purged myself from all shades, customs, and traces of negative thoughts and attitudes that contributed to my unacceptable behavior. I have participated in most all forms of self-development education to include vocational training literacy courses, certifications and I have found a strong spiritual base. This way of life has given me the tools to always communicate my best state of mind with positive energy.

I now live in the present, so I may harness the moment I reflect on my past so that I may learn from my mistakes and from them both I get foresight and direction. It was a gradual process to fall into the negative lifestyle, and just as equally, it has been a deliberate and gradual process to rid myself completely of a negative type of mindset, and at the end of this road, I so hope to find an opportunity to do the things the right and correct way from here on out.

I understand at my point of incarceration, I was a threat to public safety, and it took all of these years of growth and soul searching to find myself and to understand what true remorse is. Today, I express my deepest apologies and deepest remorse for my actions. I can say as the man I am today, I am no longer a threat to public safety, and I know there is no longer an interest of justice to keep me further incarcerated.

About the Author

Anthony Godfrey is from Berkley, CA and has been acquainted with the criminal end of the justice system since 1985. He grew up in the eighties as an adolescent (teenager) without a mother or a father present in his household. He was a product of an environment when drug trafficking and gang banging in Los Angeles was at an all-time high as he went between county jails and detention centers as a youth. Unfortunately, he eventually landed in prison. He had a 35-year prison sentence in WA state and was in from 1997 to his release in 2023. Anthony Godfrey has made some major improvements and has completely turned his life around.

Through continued progress and refinement, he demonstrates a better version of himself. Even though he has made a lot of bad choices, while incarcerated he has developed critical and independent thinking skills and is no longer influenced by the negativity. Also, he's amassed a number of credits and achievements, and one of them is writing his very own published book: *The Best Product of the Culture*.

www.ingramcontent.com/pod-product-compliance
Lightning Source LLC
LaVergne TN
LVHW010320070426
835513LV00025B/2437